To: Mi...

Your pal, Buster

Go West Young Basset

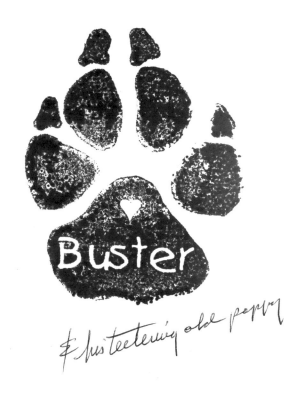

& his teetering old pappy

GO WEST YOUNG BASSET

Following the Sage Advice of Old Horace Greeley,
Buster, Together with His Old Pappy, Has Redeployed
to the High Desert in Boiseeeee, Idyhoe

The Further Exploits of a Rescued Hound

Story by Buster Appel
Related in the Lad's Own Voice

Typing by his old pappy, Walt Appel

Cover & Illustrations by Va Walker

ISBN: 1508836140
ISBN 13: 9781508836148
Library of Congress Control Number: 2015904172
CreateSpace Independent Publishing Platform
North Charleston, South Carolina

OTHER BOOKS BY BUSTER APPEL & HIS OLD PAPPY, WALT APPEL

No Mulligans, No Gimmies, No Muffelettas

Buster The Ferrari Basset - Memoirs of a Rescued Hound

Buster's Blog: buster'stwocents.com.

CONTENTS

DEDICATION

This tale of an old hound doggie coming out to live in the High Desert of Idyhoe is dedicated to all the wonderful people (maybe 5 or 6 hundred of them) whom old pappy and I have met in our less than three years here in sunny Boiseeeee, Idyhoe.

ACKNOWLEDGEMENTS

Ho, Boy, could I have remembered all this crazy stuff without those wonderful new pals out here in the boonies, as well as a bunch of folk back east, reminding me of it?

The answer is: No Way!

To be fair though, I must single out my amazing artist friend, Va. Pappy does a reasonable job of typing this stuff up for me, but without dear Va's illustrations and enhanced photos, this baby would be flat as the proverbial pancake! With her expert help, I think you will find my crazy stories begin to take on a bit of life.

INTRODUCTION

When I was just a young dog, my old pappy began recording my exploits mainly because my dear Mum, who had insisted on adopting me, just thought that I was so darned cute. She always got the biggest charge out of each of my silly antics, and she wanted to be able to share them with her family and friends back in her native land of Sweden. So, she asked old pap to write down just about everything I did all day long!

That's how I came to publish my Memoirs way back when I was only seven years old. I told old pappy that I didn't want to wait, so here I am now 10 years old, and I have decided to write a sequel because the wonderful fellow who edited my Memoirs said that it is your third book which sells the first two. Actually, *Go West Young Basset* will only be my second book, but maybe I can count old pappy's little tome, No Mulligans since he does all my typing.

Anyway, I hope you like my adventures since old pap moved us out West back in '12. Oh, yes, if you do happen to enjoy reading about me, I would appreciate your mentioning my story to Ellen, the nice TV lady, when you run into her!

CHAPTER - 1

GETTIN' OUTA DODGE.

If you read my Memoirs, which of course I hope you have, you may remember that my dear old Mum went to the Big Doggie Park in the Sky back in Aught Eight. As you might recall, she and my old pappy adopted me, and (according to Mum) rescued me from several months of bumping around in Basset foster homes. Anyway, sometime in early '12, old pap decided to put our "little dump in the city" on the market. Pap tried a realtor, Facebook, match.com, friends, and anything else he could think of, but that old house still sat there, probably because things were still depressed after the Aught Eight financial crash.

Well, old pappy was getting a tad discouraged when Rakish, the proprietor of our little neighborhood wine shop, mentioned that the shop's previous owner, Wayne, another friend of pap, mentioned that he was interested in our place. So, pap called Wayne, and within minutes they were standing in the living room agreeing on a price for the place (shades of the fortuitous sale of Mum and pappy's old house in Cockeyesville).

You see, my dear old Auntie Laurie had been bugging old pap for a couple of years to move out West and live near her. She had gone to school in Colorady and gotten to love the mountains and all that outdoor stuff, and she must have thought pappy and I would be happier out near her than living back East around her less exciting brothers. Pappy had put her off as long as possible, but she finally found us a nice little house only a block from her place which had only one floor so pap didn't need to fall down the stairs anymore.

So, old pappy was planning for us to make a real big move, dang near across the entire country, which of course required that we sell the old place and empty it out so a new owner could move in. There's another rub, emptying the old place of what appeared to be about 300 years of accumulated knick-knacks, etc. For sure, if it hadn't been for a wonderful lady named B. Bistro, we'd still be sitting back there in Charm City trying to unload our junk. This great lady was recommended to us by our dear friend, my Auntie Freddie. Miss Bistro normally helped people prepare for estate sales, but she agreed to help us pack up our household for the big transfer. Yikes, Miss B came to the house one morning dragging her big juicing machine along with a big bag of fruit and veggies, and proceeded to make a couple giant glasses of juice for herself and pap. She said she always "juiced" her Mum and herself every morning to get the day off to a swimming start. Of course, old pappy wanted to jump right aboard this healthy program, and before you know it, we have a big, old juice machine of our own.

Miss B has recently started a new juice bar right down in the Canton area of good old Charm City, and on a recent phone conversation, she reminded old pappy of a little incident about which he had completely forgotten. Apparently, old pappy and Miss B had thought that a frisky young hound doggie wouldn't be interested in being "juiced," so while they were busy discussing the house evacuation details, I decided to see just what the big deal had been with all the fruit and veggies. Darned, I was just lifting a container of strawberries out a bag that Miss B had forgotten and left on the floor. I almost had that little plastic container out of the bag when Miss B caught me in the act!

Here we are a couple years later and she still gets a big belly laugh out of my fabled curiosity!

Old pappy, as you may remember from my old Memoirs, is probably one of the luckiest dudes walking around, so now he has a sale of the old place and a great lady to pack us up and get us out of the house. Now, this winning streak just was not about to end. A neighbor put us onto a little outfit right down on 36th Street (which is also known as "The Avenue") called Cotton Duck Title Company. This wonderful little company quickly prepared all the paperwork required for the sale and transfer of our little house to old Wayne.

Got it all done and recorded for an unbelievably reasonable cost, so we could get our show on the road!

At this point, I am getting really excited, plus just a little nervous. Pappy had said that we were moving to a nice new house where I would have my own doggie door to go out and come in whenever I wanted, but it was all a little scary. Then, one day these really nice guys and a nice girl came and packed up all of our furniture and stuff. It was a really fun day 'cause the guys and girl would pet me every time I tried to see just what it was they were doing, but then I had to stay in the kitchen for a while so they could load everything into their big truck. When the movers were all done and pulled off with our possessions, old pap packed up the car with things we'd need on the trip, and we took one more look around at the old place.

Well, for our last night in Charm City, we stayed at the really neat hotel called the Colonnade which pappy used to call our little B&B down the street. Boy, was that fun! I had to sleep in the really cushy bed with pap, and we had breakfast in bed in the morning. Did ya notice? Old pappy is letting me tell the story myself this time. Since I got my own blog, I have a lot more confidence, so old pap said I could go for it! I'll tell you a little more about my blog a little later. I had been thinking about it for some time, but old pappy, being the procrastinating rascal he is, naturally took his good old time to begin typing it up for me. I'll tell you all about it when we get there.

CHAPTER - 2

THE ROAD WEST. (2400 MILES OF BAD ROAD?)

As you may have guessed, my dear old pappy's penchant for procrastination would get us into trouble despite his supernatural good luck. Originally, Auntie Freddie's hubby, my Unca Rudy, was going to ride shotgun and assist in driving across the country. Howsomever, by the time old pap got us all squared away on the house and belongings transport business, Unca Rudy had other commitments which precluded his tagging along with us. Fortunately (there's that phenomenal fate thingy again), my dear Auntie Helena agreed to fill in and help pap get us on the road. Naturally, all this positive karma threatened to be too good to be true, and, sure enough it was! Auntie Helena's driver's license was set to expire in 6 or 7 days, so the ride was not destined to be a particularly leisurely one. Still, we embarked on the 2400 mile jaunt in our relatively new

Toyota RAV4 (pap bought this car because it had the lowest rear entrance portal of any cars he had seen just so I'd be able to jump in, even as I got older) for what would turn out to be a rapid, but very enjoyable trip.

Sure, you guessed correctly again, it is entirely possible that old pappy would not have gotten us out of the state of Maryland without Auntie Helena's help, or if we did, we may have wound up driving all night looking for a motel which allows dogs! Old pap did remember to join up with triple A, and got their maps and tour guides so we would have some idea which way to go. Auntie Helena had the foresight to get the number of a terrific outfit which you can call during your driving day telling them about where you will stop that evening, and they look up a doggie friendly motel and make a reservation for you. All the places we stayed were really nice, and in each case the concierge person was able to refer us to a nearby restaurant. These eating places all turned out to be just fabulous, so old pap and Auntie Helena were able to have a very nice dinner each day. Of course, here in the good old U.S.ofA., us canines are not allowed in such establishments, but I just stayed in pappy's room and got the bed all nice and comfy for him to return. One night, I stayed in the car when the restaurant was beyond an easy walk, and pap parked where I could keep an eye on them while they were dining. Wow, the best part was sleeping right there in bed with good old pappy, though he complained a bit about my nocturnal movements.

As I mentioned, Auntie Helena's license was about to expire, so we weren't able to do a lot of sightseeing along the way, but we had lots of fun just the same. We averaged about 600 miles a day, and arrived all in one piece on the evening of the fourth day after our departure from good old Charm City.

Our spiffy conveyance.

"Efficient (and beautiful) pump attendant, Auntie Helena."

That's me on the motel bed.

Motel-henge.

Lotsa Rocks

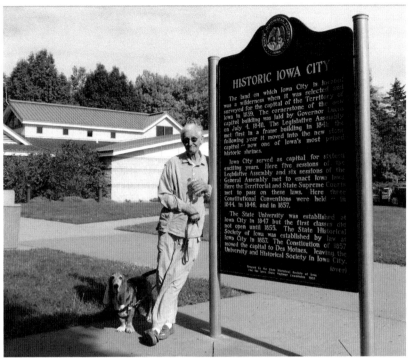

Could this pair have made it almost to the Pacific without Auntie Helena's help? Probably not!

Head of state. (Nebraska, that is.)

Lotsa Road

Auntie Helena and old pap at Dinner

CHAPTER - 3

WELCOME TO BOISEEEEE, IDYHOE.

Well, of course, we went right to my Auntie Laurie's house when we came into town, and after chatting a bit, it was decided that we should go down the block and show me and Auntie Helena the Roosevelt Market. Since this was my very first visit to Boise, I had never been to the Market before, but had heard that they keep a cookie jar inside full of doggie biscuits, so of course I was kind of anxious to check it out. As we got to the Market, Auntie Laurie wanted to

Just arrived - Delicious!!

take a photo of us all in front of the place. I wasn't particularly excited about the idea since my thoughts were on that alleged doggie biscuit stash. However, being a dutiful lad, I agreed to pose with Auntie Helena and old pap for a quick pic. As it happened, there were two young girls who had just been in the Market there also, and one of the girls had just gotten a delicious looking muffin inside. The girls wanted to get in on the photo, but pappy warned them about my "foodie" tendencies and to be very careful about the muffin. While waiting for old Auntie Laurie to get her phone camera ready, the girls were petting me, and the one with the mouth-watering muffin was holding it way out to the side, heeding pappy's caution. Naturally, the temptation was a tad too much for me, especially considering that I hadn't had a bite to eat since we had arrived.

Primping for the photo.

Shocked!

What's a hungry hound doggie to do?

The girls at the Market were sixth graders at the Roosevelt Elementary School just across the street from the Market, so they really thought that my quick move to help with the muffin was hilarious. Old pap offered to replace the muffin, but my little victim declined with a big laugh. Later on, of course, pap gave the girls copies of my exciting Memoirs in order that they could get to know me better.

So, finally we got inside the Market, and I was able to sniff out the storied cookie jar! Sure enough, there were handfuls of delicious looking doggie biscuits therein. Needless to say, the Market has been one of my favorite destinations here in town ever since

CHAPTER - 4

A HOSTILE ENVIRONMENT!

Oh, if every little thing here in good old Boise were as hospitable as the Roosevelt Market. Life is good, but not perfect, and later on while we were taking a little walk around the neighborhood, I happened to step onto a little weed growing near the sidewalk. It felt as though someone had stabbed me in the tootsie -yikes! Here's the problem - I can't stand anyone so much as touching my tender little tootsies! So, when Auntie Laurie realized that I had found what the desert-dwellers out here cheerily refer to as a "goat head," she and pappy and Auntie Helena tried to remove the offending object. Naturally, I began growling and snapping at any thing coming near my throbbing little foot. Fortunately, good old Auntie Laurie, being well practiced in such high desert emergencies, quickly removed her sweater, wrapped it around my noggin, and held me tight until the others were able to remove the "goat head." Well, let me tell you, that was quite the introduction to one of the dangers of the wild, wild west!!

By the way, I'm told that those little, old goat heads can flatten a bicycle tire! I've learned since that little episode that there are quite a few other pitfalls that one can encounter out here in the boonies, too. There are sand burrs and cockleburs, also, which are both real mean looking little sticker pods. Luckily, I haven't yet encountered any of these rascals. Old pappy is really careful where he walks with me, and also tries to watch what I'm getting into so he can redirect my attention before I get myself in that kind of trouble. Then, there is Cheat grass, sometimes called drooping brome, or by its technical name, Bromus tectorum. This grass, native to Europe, Asia, and Africa was apparently introduced to the Great and Intermountain Plains as a replacement for native grasses which were lost in droughts, and are considered good grazing grass by some ranchers. It has the tendency to get out of hand though and is accused of greatly increasing the incidence of wild fires. As far as us canines are concerned, the problem with cheat grass is the seed which opens like a tiny umbrella. If they get in your ear, they are very difficult to remove because of the little umbrella spines. Again, I've been able to avoid these suckers, thank goodness.

Thus, as you can now imagine, there are some formidable dangers for a young pup, or even a seasoned old hound dog such as my goodself out here in Sunny Boise.

Yikes!

CHAPTER - 5

THE "MARKET."

My Auntie Laurie's house and pappy's and my house, which are only a block apart, are located in Boise's "East End," and just another block from both of them is what locals refer to as "the market." Yes, that is the same place where I was able to score my first chow "swipe" out here in our new town (please refer back to chapter III). The market is a really special place, begun in the year 1900, and now operated by two dear little ladies, some of their offspring and other relatives, and rotating part-time neighbors and students. The establishment serves lunch every day and has quiches, salads, and sandwiches available for breakfast and light dinner. On weekends, the staff at the market whips up some very memorable brunches, though one mustn't be in too big a hurry.

Also, there is a quaint, albeit probably non-profitable "loss-leader" type tradition which provides free refills all day after a customer purchases the first cup of joe in the morning. Regulars still occasionally mention one former coffee aficionado, since gone on to his reward in the great doggie park in the sky, who might come in for his free refills the following day, or even two days later.

In addition to coffee and light meals, the market stocks assorted candy for the kids at the Roosevelt Elementary School across the street, ice cream and sodas, beer and wine, and grocery items in convenience quantities. The only thing missing in the market to make it feel as though you were back around the year 1900 is a pot-bellied stove with a bunch of old codgers circled about it. Actually, there are several neighbors, sometimes referred to as the "usual suspects," who tend to gather for coffee and chatter most mornings.

The Market windows are repainted for each season - note the pumpkins.

The Candy Case with that Fabled Doggie Biscuit Jar.

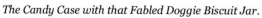

Pap and I stop by the market most mornings before our "early" walk to grab a doggie biscuit for me and a cup of what pap calls "diluted mud" for him. Old pap is unable to take advantage of the "free refills" as one cup of such swill pretty much holds him for the day. I had almost forgotten, but the wonderfully tempting baked goodies are displayed on a small table which is low enough to tempt the young school lasses and lads, or (more likely) the table may just be a leftover from the early 1900's when people were much shorter. Anyway, old pap is very careful to steer me away from that particular temptation. Breads, though, are also kept on a very low shelf, and I've been able to snag three (if I haven't lost count) of those delicious loaves. Of course, old pap then feels obliged to purchase my little prize!

Through the summer the market hosts a block party one or two times a month during which the street in front of the store is blocked off at either end of the block, and a local band is employed to provide music. This little party adds to the cohesiveness of the neighborhood and, besides, is great fun.

Recently, the ladies have obtained a license to serve beer and wine as well as sell package goods, so on nice evenings, which most are here in Sunny Boise, folks can gather on the patio before the store, and do a little socializing whilst enjoying a cold brewski.

The Market is a real neighborhood treasure and only closes about 3 days a year. Of course, when the sign goes up saying, "Market will be closed," for instance for Labor Day or Christmas, a cry goes up from the usual suspects, "You guys are closing again?"

CHAPTER - 6

OUR PLACE.

For the first several weeks that we were in Idyhoe, we had to stay at Auntie Laurie's house since our furniture hadn't made its way out here. It was fun staying there with Auntie's three doggies, Zeke, Pi, and Tator, and her four kitties. Of course, I had to be kept out of the way when everyone else was having meals due to my extreme foodie tendencies. Sometimes, we would go down to the school yard, and I could run around with the others, as long as pappy had been sure to close all the gates. We hound doggies just can't be left to mosey about on our own since we have the propensity to follow our noses which can get a person into lots of trouble. Auntie Laurie's pardner, Kim, would go with us and throw a ball to the other dogs, but I couldn't keep up with them on account of my really short legs. Sometimes Kim would give me a belly scratch so I wouldn't feel left out of all the fun.

Well, finally one day our belongings arrived with the moving guys, a different crew than the ones who packed us up back in Charm City. Guess that's why it takes a while for your stuff to cross the country. It apparently gets transferred

Auntie Lar and old pap at 823

a couple times on the trip! Anyway, we got busy setting up the furniture in the appropriate spaces, and in a few days we were all settled into our new digs.

Our house is real nice, and as I mentioned, all on one floor so that old pappy doesn't have to worry about falling down the stairs any more. We have a fenced-in back yard, and ole pap got me a doggie door installed real quickly so he didn't have to come running every time I needed a potty break. After we'd been here about 6 or

7 months, pap decided to change our yard to what the good old desert-dwellers call "zero-scape," which just means instead of grass we have pebbles and plants that can live on a minimum of water supplied by a "drip line." It is sort of close to the "desert" lawns they have down in Arizony.

Wow, inside I have my observation chair in old pappy's little office room, my crate and bed in pappy's bedroom, and another nice bed in the guest room. I almost always sleep in pappy's bedroom (just in case he might need any help)

That's me at my Sentry Post

during the night, but for my daytime naps, I have a choice of spots where I can snooze. This is a fine arrangement with one minor exception - when we have guests from back East, my guest room day-bed is usually moved to another location. Oh yes, good old pappy fluffs up all of my blankets for me several times a day.

.

CHAPTER - 7

OUR SWELL NEIGHBORS.

Old pappy and I do a lot of walking; usually at least three times a day, and invariably we run into neighbors. After being in town for just two years, I'll bet you that I have made about 3 or 4 hundred pals; so many, in fact, that old pappy has a really hard time remembering all of their names. You wouldn't believe how many people say, "Oh, I had a Basset Hound when I was a youngster, and I just love them!" It always makes me kind of proud to be a member of such a popular breed of doggie. Pappy gives everyone we meet a copy of my Memoirs, just so they can get to know me better and be wary of my foodie thingy. I don't charge anything for the books that pap gives to my friends, but I ask them to let Miss Ellen, the TV lady, know if they like my story, 'cause I figure if I can get on her show, I'll sell a bunch of books! Of course, I tell them if they don't like my book, to please just keep it to themselves.

One of our best friends here in town is a feller we met on one of our first walks around the neighborhood, Mr. Blakey. He was just coming out of his yard as we were going by, and he and old pappy got to talking and discovered that they were both beancounters. Of course, old pap hasn't done much beancounting lately since he's been retired from that activity for about 22 years, but as the old saying goes, "old accountants never die, they just lose their balance." Anyway, Mr. Blakey became a good friend of ours, and stops by after work sometimes and has a little cheese plate with old pap. I kind of like that idea because it fits right in with my food appreciation tendency. Occasionally a bit or two of that scrumptious cheese will fall my way, and it don't get much better than that!

Gosh, I'm almost forgetting Miss Karen, our next door neighbor. She is just a peach of a lady, and I feel like she is becoming another dear Auntie of mine. Actually, she is one of the first persons out here in the boonies to personally witness my fabled quickness and amazing agility when it comes to locating and retrieving people-food items (well, besides the little sixth graders at the market). Miss Karen had been to the grocery store and stopped over to help pappy with some little household chore when she placed a loaf of bread on one of our kitchen counters. By that time she should have read about the "8 inch rule" in my Memoirs and would have known not to leave so tempting an object so close to the edge of the counter. So, she may have been in a hurry or possibly had just forgotten about one of many rules necessary when in the presence of a curious and omni-hungry hound doggie. Of course, I felt obliged to take full advantage of this very interesting turn of events. A minute or two later, Miss K returned to the kitchen just as I was finishing up the bread. Being considerate, I had left a slice just in case anyone else might want a taste. Old pap and I had forgotten all about this little incident until Miss K happened to remind us of it when she and pap were engaged in a recent conversation concerning my table manners. Miss Karen also has a doggie named Lenny, a beautiful Labrador Retriever. He comes over to visit me and pap, and we both get an extra biscuit or two.

I'll tell ya, we have so many great neighbors (almost all of them have a least one nice doggie, also), that if I were to mention all of them, this here sequel would threaten to exceed the volume of good old Mr. Tolstoy's *War and Peace*. I feel confident that not even my good friends will want to slug through almost 1,500 pages of my ruminations! Howsomever, I will mention a couple of real nice ladies who live nearby our place. One is Miss Judes, who has a great puppy named, Tilly (that's short for Muttilda), and is a native Baltimoron just like old pappy. Miss Judes grew up in a nice neighborhood very near our old place in the city. She has been out here in these boonies for neigh on to 40 years, so she is almost a local and is actually one of the "usual suspects" at the market.

Then, there is Miss Tammy, who hails from Missouri and has also been here in Boise for quite a few years. She has three great doggies of her own, Buddy, Zoe, and Misty, a feisty little rascal who we found in one of the neighborhood yards. Pappy and I were at first thinking that we could adopt Misty, who we were thinking of calling, "lil booger," but we are really not capable of caring for such a sweet little critter, so Miss Tammy took her over. Miss Tammy also walks and/or baby sits lots of other neighborhood pups, as well as a kitty now and then, and she tutors neighborhood kids in math and science. I'll be telling you a bit more about Miss Tammy later on in the story.

Of course, my very favorite neighbors are my Aunties Laurie and Kimmers. As you know they only live a block and a half away from our place, so we see them very regularly. When we first got out here, they had 3 doggies (Zeke, Pi, and Tater) and 4 kitties. Last year, Zeke and Pi both went to the big doggie park in the sky, and our local rescue outfit provided Samson and Lucy to keep Tater company. For some crazy reason, Sam isn't real fond of me, and growls when I come into the house, but Auntie Laurie gives him wufo and he quiets down. On the kitty side, Tarzan and one of his sisters disappeared, and a sweet little guy named Gravy sort of bypassed the rescue and joined the family. Those guys have a really neat back yard, but when we visit, pap mostly keeps me on the leash, 'cause I like to munch on the leavings of the kitties if I get out into the yard. Auntie Lar had her lawn zero-scaped several years ago since watering grass all summer is expensive and a waste of a very precious resource.

Oh, yes, our neighbors on the other side are Miss Jenny and Mr. Tom. They are real nice, and Miss Jenny's Mom and Pop, who live in Narlins, come to visit once in a while, and then the whole crowd goes out for a little happy hour. Their dogs, beautiful black labs, are great neighbors, too, but Cooper (Coop) had to leave for the big doggie park in the sky recently. His younger Bro, Rocky, is doing his best to fill in for old Coop, though.

We also have about 8 other Basset Hounds in the neighborhood, who I'll introduce later.

CHAPTER - 8

OUR FIRST WINTER IN THE HIGH DESERT.

Ho, Boy, It really does get cold out here in the high desert! Maybe you just notice the cold more because most days when one peers out the window, the sun is shining brightly and it appears to be warm. Then, you step outside and the polar blast smacks you right in the puss!

I may have mentioned that old pappy and I (together with my Auntie Helena, of course) arrived in Boise around the middle of September. Most everyone here was expounding on how special and wonderful the Fall seasons are here in the Treasure Valley, and how much they just love this time of year. It didn't take long for old pappy and I to get the feeling that these cheerful Boise residents seem to be afflicted by what good old Mr. Greenspan once infamously called "irrational exuberance." Mr. Greenspan, the Chairman of the Federal Reserve System at the time, was referring to the stock market's buoyancy, not the weather, but you can get the idea. After we had been out here in the boonies for a while, old pap began to believe that the natives and long time residents are leaning in the direction of eternal optimism. For instance, when it gets really cold, they will say, "Oh, it never stays this cold for long, and, conversely, in summer when it hits 115 degrees, their refrain is, "Oh, it never get's this hot for long." Of course, Miss Karen and others warned us that it can snap cold in a heart beat when you near October, and our first two years bore this message out.

Actually, the beginning of our first winter in good old Boise was exciting in a way. Apparently the germ population is a bit varied from the gang we were exposed to back in Charm City. Old pappy got hit first with the Big Bad Boiseeeee Belly Buster Bug, and he couldn't get more than three feet away from the commode for a week. Then, he was just able to get us out of the house for a bit of fresh air, when the Big Bad Idyhoe Cold Bugs jumped on his case. Yikes, it was almost as bad as my meet-ups with those special Boiseeeee goat heads I mentioned back in Chapter IV.

Will Buster see his shadow today?

Will there be 6 more ~~weeks~~ months of Idahoan winter?

YES, it gets cold here.

Now, I must break the chronology of my story because we are currently heading into our third winter here in Sunny Boise, and the weather has been outstanding right up until a couple of days ago. We actually got past the first week of November with daytime highs in the 70's, and just delightful days. Why, just yesterday when the weatherman, a cheerful fellow named, "Larry," said we were going to have snow, old pappy and I were bragging to one another that it never snows more than 4 inches at a time here in Boise. Howsomever, it has snapped, and yesterday and today we've experienced a continual snowfall which has probably exceeded 8 blooming inches! Mind you, we are not talking anything like the "hundred year" snows from back in Aught Nine when we were almost trapped inside our little house back in Charm City (you may even remember that tall tale from my Memoirs), but for the high desert, this has been exciting enough! Old pappy put my Thundershirt on me and we trucked on down to the market anyway. That thunder shirt isn't worth an odor in a windstorm when we have a thunderstorm or some yahoos shooting off firecrackers, but it does feel fine when the temps are down around 5 or 10 degrees. Gosh, not even any of the usual suspects were there, so old pap and I didn't spend lots of time traversing the neighborhood.

CHAPTER - 9

SPRING COMES TO THE HIGH DESERT, AND I MADE FRIENDS WITH MISS NANCY.

Well, things are getting back to "normal," though a tad cooler than our first two Novembers here, and the "locals" are again denying that it ever gets this cold this early or snows this much in Boise. Must say when the snow finally stopped, it got nice and sunny, but the temps haven't topped 30 degrees yet, so this white stuff will be hanging around for a while.

Getting back on track, following that first uneventful winter here in Sunny Boise, Spring sort of eased into place, and old pap and I picked up our walking pace as the temps began climbing. Generally, our first walk of the day at around 7A.M. takes us several blocks to the east and then circling back around, finishes up at the market for my morning biscuit and a cup of diluted mud for pappy. As we approached the front of the market one morning, the usual suspects were already sitting at the tables outside, and I happened to snag a piece of bone (probably discarded by one of the other pups in the neighborhood). Of course, old pap started hollering at me to drop my brand new find just as we came astride the early coffee imbibers which must have alarmed Miss Nancy. Now, Miss Nancy, a founding member of the usual suspects and retired Nurse from St. Luke's Hospital, virtually sprang into action, attempting to remove the delectable morsel from my clenched jaws. Of course a hound dog-gie instinctively rejects such an idea, so in my attempt to hang onto my prize, and certainly not meaning any harm, I nailed Miss Nancy's hand. At that point, things nearly got out of control because Lucius, old Mr. Jerry's tiny dog, came after me like a Doberman, so I had to fend him off, and at the same time Mr. Jerry, fearing for little Lucius's safety, grabbed my neck lifting me right off the ground. Luckily, old pap still had hold of my leash severely limiting my movements, or I may have been tempted to detach one of Mr. Jerry's arms since it felt as though he were trying to choke me.

Me, pap, and Tarzan relaxing after my traumatic "bone" incident.

Anyway, the whole incident was over in a matter of minutes, and no more harm was done, thank goodness. Miss Nancy did have a nasty looking little gash in her hand from my reactive grab, so she went over to St. Luke's which is just a few blocks away to have it properly treated. Ho boy, such excitement first thing in the morning! Miss Nancy and I have forgiven each other and have been good friends ever since, and she even slips me an extra biscuit if she happens to be in the market when we arrive there. Miss Nancy is actually a very generous animal lover, and she feeds the squirrels who also hang around the market every morning.

CHAPTER - 10

OUR FIRST SUMMER IN THE "CITY OF TREES."

An interesting aspect of our new "hometown" is the abundance of lush green lawns and parks and big old trees lining all our streets. To the casual observer, this idyllic scene can seem very natural. Howsomever, it is not as "natural" as it looks; practically every blade of this greenery must be watered every day throughout the entire summer. You see, old Boise supposedly got it's name when, many years ago, a couple of French trappers wandering through the desert came upon what we now call the "Boise River," and seeing a few trees growing along the river, cried, "les bois, les bois." (the woods, the woods). Well, the ancestors of some of our neighbors thought it would be a good idea to run with that theme, as a modern marketeer might say, and they planted a bunch of trees all around the little town they were building and decided to call their new town,

"Boise.," with the nickname, "City of Trees!" Now, in order to keep these trees alive during the very warm desert summers, they had to devise systems of irrigation, and pap and I suppose, at some point had to dam up the spring runoff of the winter snows in the surrounding mountains in order to release the water gradually so as to last the entire summer. The present dam provides what we now call, "Lucky Peak Reservoir."

Just how the town name went from, "Bois" to "Boise," we're not sure, but old pap and I were here saying, "Boisy" for a couple years until someone finally told us the current proper pronunciation is more like, "Boy - C." Go figure!

When old pap and I arrived in September of 2012, our little house had, in addition to a large, old maple tree and several others, nice lawns in front and in back. To keep the place looking reasonable, Auntie Laurie had contracted one of the local "landscapers" to cut and trim the lawn until our arrival in town. Well, of course, it wasn't long before old do-it-yourself pappy decided that he could handle this little chore himself and went out and purchased a lawn mower. Naturally, being environmentally proper, he bought the electric model with the long plug-in cord. Just about the first time the old codger tried out that machine, he agitated a few internal body parts trying to lug the thing around while at the same time not cutting the umbilical cord in two. Most likely, that was the incident which started a rather prolonged period of physical difficulties for old pap.

So, before very long, old pap contacted a great landscape company called TLC Landscaping, LLC, and arranged with them to replace most of the grass in the back yard and all of it in the front yard to achieve our zero-scape lawn.

CHAPTER - 11

A REALLY NICE YOUNG PERSON - NOW A GRADUATE OF ROOSEVELT ELEMENTARY.

Old pappy and I met a sixth grader named Claire and her Mum one day when they were waiting for her brother, Alex, to finish shooting some baskets after school. Claire and her Mum were relaxing at the Market as old pap and I wandered by, so of course, pap had to present them with an officially pawed copy of my Memoirs. Claire thought that I was pretty cool, and asked if she could walk me a bit sometimes while they were waiting for Alex to finish up his after school activities. Well, naturally old pap was more than happy to have the help (I just love walking around the neighborhood, smelling the roses, so to speak), and most days Claire and her Mum would stop by the house and take me for an extra spin.

Claire read my Memoirs, and her Mum told old pap that she had thought my story was even better than the doggie book they made the movie from, Marley and Me. Well, you can see why Claire and I became good friends! Here is a pic of a drawing she made of me (she loves golfing):

My pal, Claire, a budding artist, put me on the green.

Well, as you can imagine, things were going swimmingly; Claire and her Mum would pick me up at the house and take me down to the school yard to meet a few of her chums, and we'd visit and walk some more. Howsomever, I guess I'm not quite as lucky as old pap 'cause I kinda messed up this sweet deal.

What happened was that one day when we went to the Vet to check on something, Dr. Steve recommended their big bones for me to chew on to help keep my teeth clean. Of course old pap purchased a couple of the frozen bones, and when we got home, he gave me one of those delectable rascals to chew out in the yard. Naturally, I wanted to bring my new goodie into the house, and after some negotiations, old pap broke down and let me bring the bone in. Now, I'm laying in the dining room just savoring that old bone when trouble popped up. Pappy, who was sitting at the dining room table, got up to go to the kitchen, but for some reason I perceived that he was going to remove my bone, so I lost it and gave him a little bite on the leg. Just like the time Miss Nancy tried to relieve me of that bone I found in front of the market, I can't seem to control my reaction sometimes when something so delectable is present.

So, to say the least, old pap was not amused at my behavior, and decided that my days of enjoying any kind of doggie bone were over! He also became concerned about letting Claire take me for walks, since he feared that if I should stumble upon a bone of some kind along the way, I could harm Claire or possibly one of her friends. As a result, old pappy told Claire that he could not let her walk me any-more. Needless to say, nobody was particularly happy about pap's decision, but I guess I really had only myself to blame. Of course, if old pappy's memory were a bit better, he would have remembered bones being somewhat problematic even while we were back in Charm City!

Claire and her Mum still stop by to see me, and sometimes they bring a little "care" package for old pap. Claire's Mum is a super soup-maker, baker, and cook. Claire is also interested in writing, and is currently contemplating starting her own blog, so if she needs any help, I'll of course be happy to aid her.

CHAPTER - 12

OLD PAPPY THINKS HE CAN LEAVE THE HOUSE WITHOUT HIS GUIDE DOG.

About a week before Christmas last year, old pappy got a bug that he needed a curio cabinet in which to house the multitude of photos of grandmonsters and great grandmonsters he's accumulated over the years. Fearful that I might be a hindrance in this nefarious shopping effort (sometimes I wonder if the old coot thinks at all), he set off to find the questionable necessity. I'm not able to certify the accuracy of this account since I wasn't present, but I'll relate it as remembered by old pap.

He'd gone to a number of furniture stores without any success, a few of which were staffed by persons unfamiliar with the item he was seeking, and was becoming a tad frustrated. One fellow referred him to a place which dealt in gently used appointments called the

"Bench Commission" which was appropriately located up in the area known as the "Bench" in Boise.

By the time old pap found and parked in front of the store, his anxiety level was just a tad elevated, causing him to exit the car and charge rapidly toward the store. Unfortunately, he encountered one of those concrete bumper thingys before reaching the store's entrance, and, flipping over a time or two, landed flat on the sidewalk. In keeping with pappy's "lucky" syndrome, two young fellows who were employed by the store, happened to notice him lying out there and hurried out to check on his condition. Helping old pap up off the ground, the lads inquired as to whether he thought he could stand on his own. Observing that his left foot was uncharacteristically pointing directly to the left, he replied in the negative, so they carried him inside the store, quickly finding a stool on which he could rest.

Immediately, peering down the aisle before him, old pap spied the very object which he was seeking; a very handsome curio cabinet! Obviously in a state of shock and feeling no pain, pap inquired about the article, and one of the fellows turned it about to give pappy a better view. Elated, old pap asked them to write up a sales ticket for him while awaiting an ambulance to arrive, advising that he would provide them with delivery instructions when he was able to leave the hospital.

On the short trip to good old St. Luke's hospital, pappy first phoned Auntie Tammy to ask her to retrieve yours truly and provide me boarding until he was able to return home. I was already very familiar with Tammy since she walked with me quite a bit when old pap was experiencing what is commonly called "sciatica" a few months earlier. Next, he called Auntie Laurie leaving her a message to ask her to retrieve our auto from in front of the "Bench Commission." Of course, good old Auntie Laurie called back to ask how it was that our car was at the Bench Commission, and discovered that pap was now being x-rayed at St. Luke's.

St. Luke's healthcare providers efficiently determined that old pappy had busted his left hip all to heck and would need a replace-ment. The emergency room was a bit over-loaded that evening, and to Auntie Laurie's displeasure, informed her and pap that he would have to wait until the next day for his new hip. Well, as it turned out, the delay was actually beneficial since the Doc on duty the next day decided that pap should receive a "total" hip replacement rather than the "partial" one suggested by the Doc from the night before.

So, here I am, visiting old pap at the Elks Rehab Hospital to cheer him up after his unanticipated surgery!

One could get the impression that my old pappy's real good luck was running a little thin when he busted his hip and had to spend his birthday and Christmas in the hospital and rehab, but, au contraire. This little "trip" encouraged him to locate a nice neurosurgeon feller who fixed his "sciatica" problem with a little microsurgery, and also to get back to a regular exercise program which he'd kind of lost due to the "sciatica." So, the crazy old rascal came out, if not quite smelling like a rose, at least in better shape!

While recovering and limbering up at the Elks Rehab, old pap had a phone call from an old schoolmate of his from back in Charm City. This fellow was visiting his son out here in sunny Boiseeeee when he observed the copy of my Memoirs at his son's home. Noting pap-

There's old pappy (and Me) on the Hospital Bed.

py's name on the cover, he inquired of his son if he knew old pap, and if the dude who typed up my little tome could possibly be his old classmate. Of course, his son suggested that he call the phone number he had for old pap. Well, on hearing that an old school chum was in town, pap invited them to come over to the Elk's for a chat.

When his old friend and son, David and Jon, arrived, they all sat down in one of the public areas, and David progressed to relate a tale from "the old days." It seems that one day at school, David mentioned to old pappy that he needed to take the test for his driver's license soon because his learner's permit was about to expire. According to David, pap replied that since he had his Dad's car at school that day, why didn't they go over to the DMV at lunchtime and get the license (at the time, the DMV was directly behind the school). So, though David had some doubts about such a plan being successful, they went over at lunchtime, and sure enough, the good folk at the DMV allowed the testing to proceed. The last step in the test is the parallel parking task, and, with old pap watching from across the street, David was having some difficulty moving the vehicle efficiently to the curb. Pap strolled over to the side of the car, and heard the officer mentioning that he was a collector of key fobs, and also that the one on pap's Dad's key was a very interesting one which he'd never seen before.

At that point, according to David (because old pappy claims he had absolutely no memory of the entire episode) pap said, "Well, if you like that key fob, and since you are helping my buddy get his license, you go ahead and take it for your collection." The point David was making in relating this tale was that he believes that without old pappy's "bribe," he would have flunked the test and not gotten his license that day!

As I mentioned, pappy claims to have no memory of the whole activity (which makes sense since it was just another school day for him), but obviously David remembered it in vivid detail (which again is reasonable since he got his driving license, a real big deal, that day)! I, of course, was not present at the time, so, can only relate the story per pap's memory of it.

CHAPTER - 13

VISITORS FROM CHARM CITY - AUNTIE FREDDIE AND UNCA RUDY!

Here comes yet one more example of that amazing pappy lucky charm. Auntie Freddie and Unca Rudy had been visiting their son, Daniell, out in Seattle, and had decided to stop to see us on their way home. What timing! That wonderful couple arrived just in time to welcome old pap back home from rehab, and of course Auntie Freddie took over immediately. She just went about shopping, fixin' us up some fine meals, and generally pampering old pappy and me to a fair thee well. Why, living in the Waldorf Astoria (before the Chinese insurance company bought it) couldn't have been any more plush!

Unca Rudy, naturally, was not going to be content just sitting around relaxing, so he fixed quite a few little things which needed repairing and which old pappy had been putting off for as long as possible. Old Unc retired from his work as a brilliant biologist a year or so ago, and decided to take up a bit of pottery and imaginative ceramic crafting as a hobby. He made this beautiful likeness of me into a stained glass medallion. He even hung it in our window so everyone coming in the front door would see it right away, or even people just walking down the street could admire it through the window.

Unca Rudy's window art.

Daisy & I relaxing by the meditation tower.

Also, Unca Rudy had found a great housewarming present for
our new pad out here in the Idyhoe boonies long before we had
even sold the old place back east. He and Auntie Freddie were on
a Springtime pond plant and fish food requisitioning trip to the old
Valley View Farms aquatic section to ready their little pond for sum-
mertime. Her name was Daisy! Daisy is a little concrete garden
sculpture of, you guessed it, a Basset Hound, and Unca Rudy knew
right away that we would love her. Well, she lay out on their deck for
several months until old pap and I were getting ready to vamoose,
and then Unc packed her up for the trip west. Auntie Freddie said
she really missed Daisy on the deck where there was a mark for quite
a while, but she's happy that Daisy has a good home here in the high
desert. The lil rascal is laying next to the structure where old pap
and I do our meditating. I think she likes it over there 'cause she is
pretty quiet by nature anyway!

Unc and Auntie stayed until after New Years, so they joined a
bunch of us for dinner over at Auntie Laurie and Auntie Kim's place.
It was great fun; we had noise makers and all to ring in the New Year,
and only had to wait until 10 o'clock to watch the old ball drop over
at Times Square (we're two hours earlier for everything out here in
the Idyhoe boonies)!

After that, everyone headed downtown to watch the First Annual
Potato Drop. Being big on taters out here, I guess the city decided
it would be fun to get everyone together down in the "grove" at mid-
night and have a giant potato being lowered to the ground from

about 30 or 40 feet in the air. Actually, it wasn't all that terribly impressive, but the crowd seemed to get a kick from the festivities, and they are promising to do an even bigger and better tater drop this year.

Well, as I've learned over my almost 10 exciting years, all happy visits have to come to an end to wait for the next time, and Unca Rudy had to get back to his newfound avocation, and Auntie Freddie wanted to get back to her Volunteer job as a docent at the old Baltimore Museum of Art. I sure wish I was going back to Charm City with pappy next Spring so I could see them again. Hopefully, they will be back out west here again soon, though, and I'm sure we'll have a good time again.

CHAPTER - 14

GOT MY VOICE BACK!

Geez, tonight I was feeling really tired and grumpy, maybe due to what old pap has begun calling the "interminable inversion." That's something I have forgotten to mention until now about "sunny" Boise. You see, the eternal optimists out here in the high desert mentioned the first winter we were here the thing they call an "inversion." This is an atmospheric phenomenon which occurs when warm air gets trapped somehow under cold air here in the Treasure Valley. The result is very cloudy and damp weather, and not very nice air quality. Well, of course, the usual suspects and all the other optimists here in Boise told us that these "inversions" only last a few days, and it seems that was the case for our first two winters, if we are remembering correctly. This year, however, we've already had several of those buggers, and the current one has lasted since the first of the month. Let me tell you, these unfriendly conditions can really cause a feller to get just a tad depressed, leading to a bit of grumpiness!

Got off on a little tangent there; I was going to tell you about how I got my great voice back after sort of forgetting it for a while when we came out west. I guess the long trip driving out here to Idyhoe and all the new things here like our new house, my doggie door, the Market, all the people and doggies we meet on our walks, and everything just confused or upset me. Anyway, for a time I forgot how swell it was back in Charm City to just bark and bark and bark until old pappy was ready to ask the vet if he could put a little muffler on my vocal cords. Pappy didn't really notice how relatively quiet I had gotten until I sort of found my voice again. Now that I have gotten back in tune again, so to speak, he's beginning to think about calling the vet again.

Auntie Karen, who as you know lives right next door, noticed that I had regained my mojo before old pappy, perhaps because without his hearing aids, pap can't hear much of anything! Sometimes when I slide on out my doggie door while pappy is asleep, I'll look around the yard and give a few barks just for good measure. Of course, this nocturnal music has disturbed Auntie K, and

Sheppy and I practicing back in the day!

she will holler out at me to please SHUT UP! Being the gentle and considerate fellow, I have minded her admonitions, but she still says it's a good thing she likes old pappy!

So, mostly now I try to limit my best voice to use indoors where it is less disturbing to the neighbors. Pappy says I am right back to my best barking voice as he described it in my Memoirs, i.e., when I'm hungry, or need a belly rub or any other kind of attention. Of course, barking at passers-by is not nearly as much fun as before old Sheppy went to the big doggie park in the sky, and we could harmonize our howling and barking to achieve maximum effectiveness. So, now I personally don't believe "the voice" is quite as incessant as when old pap related it to Attention Deficit Disorder (ADD). Back in my Memoirs, he said that in my case, the deficit was not related to my attention, but rather to the attention of everyone else who I met.

CHAPTER - 15

MY DEAR AUNTIE HELENA CAME TO VISIT.

Oh boy, I hadn't seen Auntie Helena since she and pappy drove me all the way out here to the high desert. What a surprise when old pap said that she was coming to see us, and bringing her new friend, Steve, along. I better tell you what happened with Auntie Helena before relating her visit this past summer. You see, my Unca Tomas was stricken by a terrible cancer like my dear old Mum a few years before. He was treated for the cancer, and for a while thought he had been cured, but, just as in Mum's case, his tumors returned, much worse. He died over a year ago, leaving Auntie Helena and their doggie, Nisseh, out in the country in their new house. Not long after, Nisseh died, also, very suddenly. Auntie Helena has had way more grieving than any person should need to bear, but, fortunately, her strong spirit has enabled her to survive and recover. She is a wonderfully positive person, and old pap and I love her very much.

After some time, Auntie met a very nice fellow named Steve, who happens to be an avid golfer, and I imagine that finding someone to help her get out on the old links was a very healing recipe for her. Anyway, back in September, I think it was, she and Steve came on out to see me and pap. Boy, we had a great time showing them all around good old Boise (when Auntie helped us drive out here to the boonies back in 2012, if you recall, she had to get right back to old Charm City because her driving license was about to expire). So, she hadn't seen hardly any of our new town and the great restaurants and places to walk here. While she and old Steve were here, Aunties Laurie and Kim and pappy took them up to the hot springs swimming pool, which they said was very nice. Of course, as usual, doggies aren't allowed up there, so I can't personally vouch for the place.

Also, while they were here we had a couple great barbecues which I am particularly interested in since there is always a chance that some choice tidbits are apt to slip off the table to within easy reach. In a situation such as this, a doggie doesn't even need to scurry up onto the table to score a couple of nice treats. Gosh it was really nice to have Auntie Helena and Steve visit, even though I wasn't able to be with them the entire time. Of course, old pappy will be sure to see them when he visits back East this Spring, but, unfortunately, I won't be going along since I refuse to travel in stowage on these silly airlines. I'm sure they will be back to visit us out here in the boonies soon again.

I hadn't mentioned old pap's plan to visit "the boys and families," all his old neighbors and pals on the east coast, and my dear old Mum's relatives in good old Sveden. He says that he wants to get back to visit all those folks before he kicks off and heads for his dubiously deserved "reward!" Well, as I mentioned, I ain't flyin' in any luggage compartment, so I'll be staying with my Auntie Tammy. Naturally, I sure won't mind staying with her and Buddy and Zoe and Misty, but I will miss old pappy. He's promised to complete the typing on this here sequel before leaving for the trip, and he'll also be able to post my blogs while he's away.

CHAPTER - 16

MY NEPHEW JD, COMES OUT TO BOISE STATE UNIVERSITY

My Unca Jim and Auntie Di's son, JD, decided to come out to good old BSU to study Accounting, of all things (he is thinking of becoming a beancounter just like my old pappy was once-upon-a-time). Anyway, his whole family has been out at one time or another to check out the school with him, or to get him settled into a dorm out at the school. His little sister Amanda came out with his Mum, Di, and really liked my and pappy's meditation tower.

JD had originally planned to live with old pap and me, but the gang back east convinced him to start out in the dorm so as to get to know the ropes and his fellow students more quickly. Actually, it is a good thing for pap and me, too, that he is living in the dorm since 18 year-old and 79 year-old schedules are quite dissimilar. Also, JD enjoys watching football and basketball on TV, activities which 'bout drive me nutz. An old doggy's ears are not sufficiently hardy to withstand such rackets!

Anyway, we all get together for meals and camaraderie regularly, marveling at a young college student's capacity for devouring his sustenance. JD stayed with old pap and me during the Thanksgiving school break which was real nice since I got quite a few extra belly scratches!

CHAPTER - 17

MY BLOODY BLOG

Golly, that reminds me, I haven't mentioned my Blog yet! You see, my crazy old pappy is always reading all sorts of "news" items, and being an old beancounter, he can hardly believe the shenanigans happening today, both in the financial area as well as the greater world. So, he's always complaining and worrying over what's to happen to our dear old country, and everybody

Sherpas removing trash from Mt. Everest! One of my early blogs on the Environment described the trashing of Mt. Everest by inexperienced "climbers" with more money than brains!

else, too. So, one day, I said, "pap, we aught to stop fretting and try to do something about it," and that's how we decided to start a blog, writing about politics, the economy, and beer. Don't ask me how we came up with this program mix, 'cause neither me nor old pap know a thing about the first two, though pap's had some experience with the last one.

Anyway, we started this blog called "buster'stwocents.com" and try to post an entry on it once a week. I do most of the research and thinking while old pappy does all the typing. My big old paws were all right on the old manual typewriter, but these teensy computer keyboard letters are just too danged close together, and I wind up with an unreadable mess. Gosh all to heck, I almost forgot. We found a wonderful gal in the neighborhood to help old pap "Post" my blogs. That's now my Auntie Juta, who used to live at Auntie Laurie's house when we first got here in sunny Boiseeeee. Auntie Juta is very smart about these 'puters and stuff, and she's real nice to me when she comes over to help post my Blog. She had a wonderful doggie named, Sophie, who would come with her sometimes, but sadly, Sophie had gotten very old and had to go to the Big Doggie Park in the Sky a couple months ago. Auntie Juta is now the Executive Director of the Boise Hive, a wonderful facility for helping local musicians practice together and record their music. We've heard rumors that she may be adopting a new puppy!

You probably already know how confusing the political situation is in our good old U.S.of A., and how those crazy politicians have somehow gotten us regular folk to kind of distrust each other like they do.

Old pap and I have decided to rename those pol's "parties" since they both seem to be doing the same dumb things, just in different ways.

We're calling them Republicrats and Demoblicans now, 'cause, as the Brits might say, there isn't a "farthing's worth" of difference between them.

So, anyway, old pappy and I are beginning to think that we probably need a whole new approach to selecting our representatives who go to our State Capitals and certainly for those who go down there to Washington, D.C. We'll

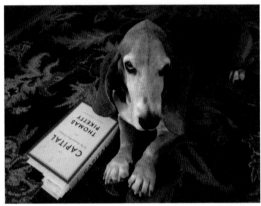

I'm reviewing Ol' Tom's hefty tome.

be discussing our ideas on my Blog for a while to see if any other good old Amuricans feel the same way, and may want to try to do something to improve things. When you check out my Blog, please be sure to let us know your thoughts.

Writing and publishing the blog is lots of fun and allows for great camaraderie between old pap and me. Here's me while studying young Tom Piketty's recent book called, *Capital in the 21st Century:*

CHAPTER - 18

UNCA JEFF AND AUNTIE NAN'S VISIT.

Gosh, here I am runnin' on all about my crazy Blog and all, and getting ready to forget to mention the great visitors who brought us some swell crab cakes from good old Charm City. Unca Jeff's business is always slow in the winter time, so he can hop a plane and come out to spend a few days with pap and me. This year, he brought Auntie Nan along and she brought a big old box of her famous chocolate chip cookies. They also brought a dozen great big Pappas crab cakes packed in with those little frozen cooler packets. Now, I understand that all those goodies are mighty fine eatin', but, unfortunately, they are not considered "dog" food! When that crazy old dude, whoever he was, said that life ain't always fair, he knew what he was talking about. I know chocolate is supposed to be bad for doggies, but I never heard anything like that about crab cakes.

Anyway, Aunties Laurie, Kim, Karen, Makenzie, and Janet, plus my hard-studying BSU nephew, JD, all came over, and pappy, Unca Jeff, and Auntie Nan all whumped up a big old surf and turf dinner with regular and sweet 'tator fries and pap's infamous veggie salad. Auntie Laurie brought a chocolate (there's that word again) pie, and also a tiramisu cake. Ho Boy, did that gang chow down. Luckily, Aunties Laurie and Kim brought their pups, Tator, Samson, and Lucy along, so I had some company, plus we mutts got us a couple of my special sensitive tummy biscuits!

While they were here, Auntie Laurie took the gang up to Idyhoe City to the hot springs spa where they had a swimmingly good time. Pap and I stayed home since they don't allow dogs (surprise) and old pap is a tad concerned about exposing his damp bod to chilly February breezes. As I mentioned earlier, pappy went up to the hot springs last summer when Auntie Helena and her bud, Steve were here visiting.

Unca Jeff approved of our "zero-scaped" yard, really appreciating the stone work, of which of course, he knows a great deal. It was supposed to rain, or more accurately here in the high desert, drizzle all weekend, but amazingly, we had really beautiful weather for their entire visit, and were able to enjoy the outdoors. So far this February, we have had unusually warm days, mostly reaching 60 degrees, while back east the mean old arctic vortex has been freezing and snowing all over those poor guys. Old pap is hesitant to call our many pals back there; our weather has been so embarrassingly loverly!

On Sunday morning, we all assembled down at the Market for what pap and I are calling the photo shoot of the Hounds of the Boiseeeeeville. My wonderful artist pal, Va, has embellished the main photo for next week's Walentine's Day celebration.

Then, we dropped Unc and Auntie off at the areoport early on Monday morning, and they were heading back to the deep-freeze, hopefully savoring their beautiful long weekend in sunny Boiseeeee.

The Boiseeeee Valentine Basset Hounds

CHAPTER - 19

HOW WE GOT OUT HERE, AND PAP'S UPCOMING TRIP BACK EAST, AND THE FUTURE HERE IN BOISEEEEE.

Well, as they used to say in Vaudeville, "When you're done yer dance, ya better get off the stage before ya get yanked off." So, I'm getting ready to wrap up this here sequel. Pappy's getting tired of typing, anyway!

First, though, I must explain a bit about how we got out here in the high desert boonies of Boiseeeee, Idyhoe. You may remember I mentioned that my dear old Auntie Laurie had "encouraged" old pappy to move out here to live near her for a while. When she graduated from Colorady State, as an Occupational Therapist, she did a couple internships back in Charm City, and then found employment in Moscow, Idyhoe. My dear old Mum and old pappy visited her up in Moscow a couple times, and on one visit they all went to Seattle and then over to San Juan Island, which according to pap was very nice. Then, about 15 years ago she moved down here to Boiseeeee. After a year or two, she bought a house here, and then expanded it so that her Mom, Marge who was having many health problems, could come and live with her. It wasn't too long before Marge's health was bad enough that Auntie Laurie was unable to keep her living at home, and she moved into the assisted living facility a couple blocks away. Old pap knew how busy Auntie Lar was with her work, and he felt that he and I moving here could be a help in visiting Marge at the nursing home. As it turned out only several weeks after we got to town, Marge decided that she'd had enough and declined rapidly and passed away. Auntie Laurie thinks she was just waiting for pap to get here to take over the responsibility for looking after her little girl.

About 8 years ago, old Auntie opened her own little clinic. She works mostly with little kiddos, ages zero to three or four, and even some kids up into the teens, as well as some adults. She has built and expanded that little clinic until now she has about a dozen helpers working there with her. Of course, each time she expands, the rent is higher, so she has to work even harder to pay the rent! She called the clinic "The Lotus Tree," and it is truly a wonderful place where, as her web site explains, "there is a place that champions every child AND every adult — where they feel not only accepted, but celebrated. This is a safe place to try new things, to meet new friends, and to explore individual avenues of expression."

Old pappy has met some of the kiddos and their parents, and has heard such glowing reports about the wonders of the Lotus Tree that he often can barely hold back a torrent of tears of pride and joy. To say that old pap is very proud of my old Auntie Laurie would be a real big understatement!

Where the senses come into play!

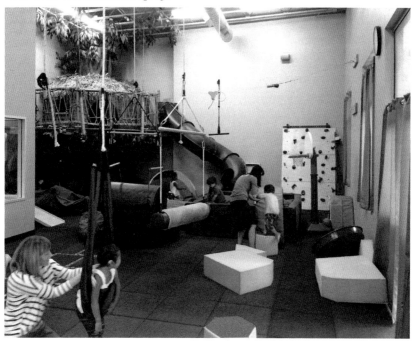

Depicted above are the Lotus Tree entrance and the "Gymnasium" where the "kiddos" learn to do all the things that other kids can do!

Now, Auntie Laurie works just like a mad scientist, but she also, together with her pardner Auntie Kim, is very generous in sharing their home with friends and neighbors. Old Auntie Lar even coaches the Boiseeeee Nemesis Ladies Rugby Team (she used to play, but I think she may be getting just a tad too old for such an "enthusiastic" sport). Auntie Kim is a Librarian at the College of Western Idaho, and is a veritable genius at all the electronic thingys that are so ubiquitous nowadays. She's always fixing old pappy's cell phone, but he is so clueless that he can never remember what she tells him to do if this or that happens to the crazy thing. Now, Auntie Kim is, as they say, "in a family way," and they are expecting a little baby girl in June. Looks like I'm gonna be a proud uncle, again!

Old pap's going to make a trip back East this Spring (Yikes, Spring is only a little over 3 weeks away) to visit Auntie Laurie's less attractive brothers and their families. While he's there, he'll slide up and down the coast a bit to visit friends who have moved in

Dinner at the Locavore Restaurant near the Lotus Tree

one direction or the other. I'll be staying here in good old Boiseeeee with my Auntie Tammy; there ain't no way you'd find me in the cargo bin of one of those drafty aircraft.

Pap's original plan was to visit everyone on the East Coast and then jump on over the puddle to see my Dear Old Mum's family in Sweden, but Aunties Laurie and Kim convinced him to make two separate trips.

That way he won't be gone for so long in one spell which could easily wear the old codger out, plus he'll be back here in good old Boiseeeee in time for the new arrival! So, I'll be missing old pappy for a few weeks each trip, but I'll be fine here in town with all my Aunties and pals around, and I'll be able to keep an eye on our place. You better believe I'll be putting the guilt trips on him for a couple extra biscuits when he gets back, too!

My little Bar and Grill on Broadway Street.

We've got the house and garden in good shape now, so when pappy returns from his travels, I'm thinking he and I will do a lot of wandering around town, sometimes pushing a little carriage along, and relaxing in the good old garden counting up the royalties coming in from my exciting sequel!!

Thanks for bearing with me, your faithful correspondent, Buster.

AFTERWORD

Well, you guessed correctly yet again; my old pappy did not complete typing this little sequel before he left town for his little "Eastern Jaunt." He is back now, and is feverishly putting the finishing touches on the typing job.

He tells me that he had a wonderful time visiting my Aunty Laurie's less exciting brothers and their families, his newest great-grand babies, his old Bro-in-law, Uncle Walt, and Shelly down in Orlando, and his dear old neighbors and friends in Charm City and elsewhere in the East. It would take a whole other book to try to relate his exhilarating tales of his adventures back there, and it, of course, would only be hearsay since I was not present for any of it!

Hence, feel free to ask him about his trip anytime you feel you have the fortitude to listen through any of his oft-embellished stories.

Our brand new Idyhoe grand baby has yet to make her grand entrance, but we think she will be called "Scout," and soon bring a measure of cheer to this old desert.

Well, got to make a "correction" already: Scout has arrived, with a fanfare reminiscent of the Beaujolais Nouveau! Her Mums, Aunties Kim and Laurie, were all prepared for an at home birth with a special "birthing pool" and all, but she was a tad late making her exciting appearance. We were anticipating her doing the doggie paddle in the pool when she finally arrived, but due to a legal rule here in Idyhoe, the whole process had to be moved over to St. Lukes Hospital (yes, that's the same place old pap got his new hip; lucky thing we all live so close). Anyway, very rapidly after the transfer, lil Scout decided to make her move, and a totally natural birth was consummated! As we go to press, the kid is growing like a weed, and smiling and laughing as if to say, "Wow, you people are sure funny looking!"

Despite the fact that this stuff is becoming old hat to me (I now have 6 nieces and nephews, and 3 grand ones), this little girl promises to be an amazing experience for old pap and me. Possibly due to the fact of her proximity to our little abode here in the high desert of Boiseeeee.

Who knows, I may need to wake old pappy up so we can begin scribbling a sequel to this here sequel?

ABOUT THE AUTHOR

The Author is a ten-year old Basset Hound who at the tender age of one year was assigned to the care of Christina and Walt Appel by the Basset Rescue of Old Dominion (BROOD), where he had lived with foster parents for most of his young life. He wrote his Memoirs at the tender age of 7 years, and decided this sequel was necessary to chronicle his move west.

The Author Went West.

The Author in the Garden

ABOUT THE TYPIST

The typist, walt appel, is better-known as Buster's old pappy, and spends most of his time typing up Buster's blog, buster'stwocents. com, when not walking with the author around and about the charming little community known as "The East End" in Boiseeee, Idyhoe.

ABOUT THE ILLUSTRATOR

The illustrator, Virginia Walker, professionally known as Va, is a beautiful lady who spent most of her life creating, together with her husband, Steve, amazingly wonderful murals for institutions and individuals. Please refer to "The Illustrators" Section of my Memoirs for more information.

49675223R00052

Made in the USA
Charleston, SC
01 December 2015